LIFE AFTER LOSS

30 Days of Hope for Moms Grieving after Miscarriage

JOINNÉ CHANDLER

Life After Loss: 30 Days of Hope for Moms Grieving After Miscarriage

Library of Congress

ISBN: 979-8-218-51300-9

Cover Design: Joinne' Chandler

Interior Design: Joinné Chandler, Toki Creative

Book Photography: Kiki Smith Photography

Image: Isabel Poulin

JOURNEY TO IVY

The rainbow that I have put in the sky will be my sign to you and to every living creature on earth. It will remind you that I will keep this promise forever. When I send clouds over the earth, and a rainbow appears in the sky, I will remember my promise to you and to all other living creatures.

- Genesis 9:12–15 CEV

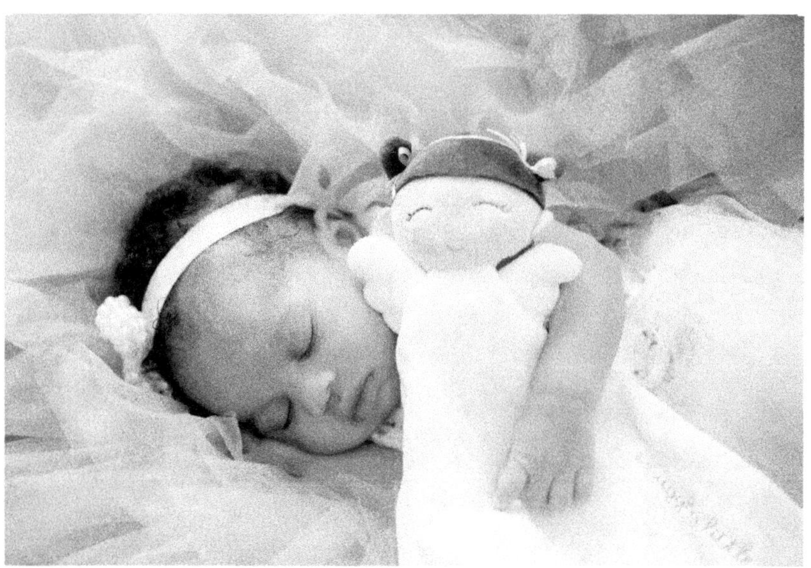

Credit: KiKi Smith Photography

DEDICATION

This book is dedicated to our three earthly babies and our one heavenly baby, Journey.

Journey, I had no idea when we learned that we were pregnant that my time with you would be so short. Yet God had other plans. He knew that you would prepare the way for your sister Ivy.

Journey, thank you for being the rainbow in the cloud for your sister Ivy. I can't wait to meet you in heaven one day.

◇◇

For you created my inmost being; you knit me together in my mother's womb. I praise you because I am fearfully and wonderfully made; your works are wonderful, I know that full well.

—Psalm 139:13–14 NIV

ACKNOWLEDGEMENTS

Infant loss is something no one wants to experience, but it has revealed the strength of God to me in ways I couldn't possibly have imagined before.

Thank you to my husband, Emmanuel, my rock. Thank you to my family and friends for their tremendous support in praying for me and keeping me accountable to finish this devotional for someone else.

Thank you to my spiritual leaders, Bishop Michael Dantley, Pastor Carol Dantley and Apostle Bertha F. Terry.

Thank you to my heavenly Father for carrying me through what I thought would be an insurmountable loss.

Thank you to my parents and parents-in-love for their support both then and now.

May our family's journey be the rainbow in your cloud.

Table of Contents

INTRODUCTION

The Bible is filled with women who have suffered loss.

Hannah bore the shame of infertility.

Ruth and Naomi lost their husbands.

Moses' mother lost her son while saving

his life at the same time.

Eve lost God's presence.

Miriam lost her brother.

Mary lost her Son.

While their stories are different, their lives were similar. They experienced what appeared to be insurmountable losses, but through the grace and favor of God, they experienced life after loss. My prayer as you read this daily devotional is that you truly will experience life after loss. That you will begin to hope again, smile again, and trust God in new ways. I pray that while your weeping may endure for a night, joy will come in the morning. Everyone's morning looks and feels different, but rest assured, God will not leave you there—He will bring you life after loss.

COMPLETE HEALING

The Sun of Righteousness shall arise

With healing in His wings;

And you shall go out

And grow fat like stall-fed calves.

—*Malachi 4:2b NKJV*

It was just the other day that I realized I hadn't been myself for three months. And I had been using my job to hide that fact from myself, pouring everything into my work at the expense of my family and other obligations.

Why had I been doing this? Because three months ago, my baby was supposed to be born. And yet it wasn't until just a week ago that I realized the source of my drive was my need to cover feelings that I didn't realize I still had. That's the funny thing about grief. It comes at the most unexpected times. It comes when you're going about your day, doing things for others or doing things for yourself.

It wasn't until my time in prayer that the Lord revealed to me the reason I had been working so hard. I had been working so hard to cope—to cope with feeling like a failure. I felt I had done something wrong and was no longer able to control my situation.

The Bible says that you can cast the load of your cares upon the Lord, and He will care for you *(1 Peter 5:7)*. There's beauty in this simplicity. Cast the load of your cares upon the Lord, and He will care for you as you go about your day-to-day.

PRAYER STARTER:

Lord, in silent moments of grief, please help me to cast the load of my cares on You. When I feel out of control, help me trust Your sovereign will.

TRACES OF GOD

Be not forgetful to entertain
strangers: for thereby some have
entertained angels unawares.

—*Hebrews 13:2 KJV*

I was getting my car serviced just after I'd learned that there was a fifty-fifty chance I was miscarrying. There at the car dealership, the female technician helping me shared that she too had gone through a miscarriage. During that whole period of time, in fact, God continually showed me traces of Himself. He reminded me through a simple statement—"that happened to me, too"—that I was not alone. There was never anyone I shared my story with who did not respond that either they had also had a miscarriage, or they had a loved one who had. Sharing my story was part of my healing. In hindsight, I saw that God always made sure there was someone in my path—an angel.

I'm grateful that even during times of grief, the Lord always makes sure He doesn't leave us comfortless. Just as He told the disciples prior to His death that He would not leave them comfortless (John 14:18), He does the same for us.

PRAYER STARTER:

Lord, even as I grieve, please help me see You in subtle ways—whether it's a simple smile, encouraging word, or someone who has experienced what I have experienced. Help me to remember that You will not leave me comfortless and that You are right here with me in my grief.

ONE IN FOUR

One in four women have experienced infant loss. Let that sink in: one in four. That means you are NOT ALONE. The likelihood of someone in your circle having experienced miscarriage is high, yet it can be one of the most isolating forms of grief. Sometimes only the mom who lost her baby may know about that loss. Sometimes, only the mom and spouse or partner may know.

As you embark on this phase of your journey, know that:

- You're not alone (Deuteronomy 31:6, Hebrews 13:5).

- You will hope again (Proverbs 23:18, Romans 12:12).

- God will give you beauty for ashes, and a garment of praise for the spirit of heaviness (Isaiah 61:3).

- It's okay not to be okay.

- Your great High Priest knows what you have need of, even when you don't (Hebrews 4:14–16).

- You have a Comforter (John 14:16).

- You are fearfully and wonderfully made, and there is nowhere you can escape from God's presence (Psalm 139).

Believe it or not, you will also feel joy again.

Lord, as I embark on this unexpected journey, please be with me. I pray that Your presence would overtake my sorrow. Please help me to feel You near me and to know that my story is not over. May my sorrow turn to joy and my mourning to dancing, in Your name. Amen.

Day 4

BROKENNESS

So I went down to the potter's
house and saw him working with
clay at the wheel. He was making
a pot from clay. But there was
something wrong with the pot. So
the potter used that clay to make
another pot. With his hands he
shaped the pot the way he wanted
it to be.

—Jeremiah 18:3–4 ERV

Have you ever tried to break something and put it back together again? It isn't that easy, is it? Sometimes it's much easier to replace it with something new, rather than repairing it. But God doesn't see things that way. He delights in broken pieces. Brokenness provides new ways for God to reveal Himself to us and make something even more beautiful.

The Bible says that God is close to the brokenhearted and those that are of a contrite spirit (Psalm 34:18). Brokenness is attractive to God, and He delights in bringing beauty from ashes (Isaiah 61:3). He delights in our broken places—we don't have to hide them from Him or from ourselves. It's in the brokenness that we learn that God doesn't throw us away. In fact, our brokenness becomes a canvas for His next masterpiece.

I've never felt more broken than when we lost our child. I was fragile, uncertain, and unsure how I would get through it. Yet, in those moments before I went to bed each night, when tears began to fall down my face, I didn't know God was closer to me than I realized.

You will not always feel this way. Take heart, because beautiful things always come out of broken pieces.

PRAYER STARTER:
Lord, please help me to embrace my broken pieces. Thank You for delighting in my brokenness. Please don't leave me here. Please help me to find comfort in Your love.

Day 5

TEARS

You have taken account of my
wanderings;

Put my tears in Your bottle.

Are they not recorded in Your
book?

—Psalm 56:8 AMP

Tears. They come at the oddest times, when you least expect them. One minute you can be totally fine. The next minute, tears just begin streaming down your face. This often happened to me in the morning or at the end of the day as I was going to bed. I remember being in the parking lot of my dentist's office when the hospital that did my DNC called to see how I was doing. I told them I was fine, which was true at that moment. Then, ten minutes later, tears began to stream down my face in the dentist's office, and continued for more than twenty minutes. There was nothing I could do but let them fall. The hygienist asked if I was okay, and I told her I wasn't.

Psalm 56:8 gives me a tremendous amount of comfort. Not only does God see us when we cry, He bottles our tears. One by one, He catches them. Every single one of them. I can imagine God having countless bottles in heaven with our names on each of them.

Tears also have cleansing and draining properties. When they don't fall, our bodies have adverse reactions. They're our bodies' way of releasing pain.

So, what do you do when the tears fall? Let them fall. Rest in knowing that our sovereign God sees and knows not only the number of hairs on our heads, but the number of tears that fall from our eyes. He catches them too. There's not a tear that falls that He does not record.

PRAYER STARTER:

Lord, help me to be okay with the tears that fall. Help me to rest in the fact that You see them and bottle them. Please give me comfort during this tremendously hard season in my life. With every tear that falls, allow your healing to flow through me. Amen.

Day 6

HOPE AGAINST HOPE

Even when there was no reason
for hope, Abraham kept hoping—
believing that he would become the
father of many nations. For God
had said to him, "That's how many
descendants you will have!"

—Romans 4:18 NLT

Have you ever felt there's no reason to hope? Have you ever felt so low that hope seemed completely absent? If you've experienced any form of loss, you've likely experienced this.

Trigger alert: Sometimes hope fails and trust must guide you. I remember being told my baby didn't have a heartbeat. I'm not quite sure what was said after that point, but I do remember that they were going to give me one week to determine if a heartbeat could be detected. Against hope I clung to hope, knowing that if God brought Lazarus back from the dead, surely He could bring my baby's heartbeat back to life. But God chose differently.

In those moments when all hope was lost, and the heartbeat was not confirmed, hope once again beckoned me to cling to it. Did I want to? Not entirely. When hope fails, that's where trust steps in. Trust doesn't force you to expect the outcome will change, but it invites you to know that you will make it through this because nothing catches God by surprise.

PRAYER STARTER:
Lord, I'm in a hopeless situation right now. I don't understand why You chose differently than I would have. When I can't hope, help me to trust Your plan.

SUPPORT SYSTEM

But Moses' hands became heavy;
so they took a stone and put it
under him, and he sat on it. And
Aaron and Hur supported his
hands, one on one side, and the
other on the other side; and his
hands were steady until the going
down of the sun.

—Exodus 17:12 NKJV

You never know how much you need them until you need them. My support system checked on me daily, and I was so glad they did. Life is not meant to be walked alone, even during the most trying times.

There's such beauty in the passage from Exodus quoted above. The children of Israel were in desperation in the wilderness when they encountered an enemy—the Amalekites. As long as Moses' arms were raised, the children of Israel were victorious (verse 11). When he lowered his arms, they were defeated. Moses, who grew tired, needed additional support for the children of Israel to remain victorious. Aaron and Hur, his support system, did just that, holding up Moses' hands to make sure they would remain raised.

The people in our support systems not only meet the needs they see, but they are also there in times of desperation when it may seem that we can't keep fighting. God always surrounds us with those who keep us encouraged and uplifted during our time of need. You do not have to do this alone.

Ask the Lord to reveal the support system He's put in place to help you persevere. They'll become the very Aaron and Hur that you need.

PRAYER STARTER:
Lord, please help me to trust the people You've brought into my life. Help me to not feel like I need to hold up all this weight on my own. Thank You for my victory.

THE RESIDUAL EFFECTS

At the moment I have all I need—
and more!…And this same God
who takes care of me will supply all
your needs from his glorious riches,
which have been given to us in
Christ Jesus.

—Philippians 4:18a, 19 NLT

Grief comes in the most surprising ways. You will think you're past the "hard part," when suddenly…BOOM, it hits you. Or you can be engaging with new and exciting parts of your life, when you realize you're struggling with something "old." Or perhaps you're having thoughts about something you've "gotten over," only to realize grief has brought back to the surface the thing you thought you overcame.

For me, the struggle has with been trusting God. As a young child, I knew there was nothing God could not do. In fact, I would trust Him for really big things and then I'd see Him bring them to pass. I knew He was my Father, and He would take care of me. He's that kind of God. Yet, doubt can begin to seep in through life's unexpected twists and turns.

When you realize you are having one of those moments where the things you never questioned about God you now do, acknowledge where you are and ask Him to remind you what you once knew. He is a rewarder of them that diligently seek Him.

PRAYER STARTER:

Lord, I've lost my way. The things I've known to be true about You, I now doubt. Please restore my confidence in our relationship and remind me of what I once knew. Thank You for being with me through every phase of grief, including doubt and fear. Reassure me that You are who You say You are.

A YEAR LATER

Now to Him who is able to keep
you from stumbling,

And to present you faultless

Before the presence of His glory
with exceeding joy,

To God our Savior,

Who alone is wise,

Be glory and majesty,

Dominion and power,

Both now and forever.

Amen.

—Jude 24–25 NKJV

One year later, as my husband and I reflected on our miscarriage, he told me that I was strong. Simple words with a profound impact: You are strong. At the time I felt anything but strength. In fact, I remember waking up the day of my DNC and being driven to the hospital—the same hospital where we delivered our two oldest children. The drive of anticipation that we'd experienced so happily before was now a drive of dread. As we got closer, more and more tears flooded my face. I felt anything but strong.

As I reflect on the Scripture passage above, what I love most is that it takes the focus off us and puts it on God. Our weakness cannot compare to His strength. In fact, His grace covers our weakness and makes us sufficient (2 Corinthians 12:9). The next time you're feeling weak or like you are falling, rest in the promise that God makes us strong, even when we don't have that strength in ourselves.

PRAYER STARTER:

Lord, despite what I'm facing today, may I rest in the fact that Your strength is all I need. Your grace is sufficient for me, and You will keep me from falling. Help my unbelief and please remind me that I'm strong because of You.

Day 10

EMOTIONAL LOSS

And He said to me, "My grace is
sufficient for you, for My strength
is made perfect in weakness."
Therefore, most gladly I will rather
boast in my infirmities, that the
power of Christ may rest upon me.

—2 Corinthians 12:9 NKJV

I remember crying when my husband and I were intimate after we lost our baby. Suddenly, the loss would hit me and become too much to bear. He would comfort me and wipe my tears away. I often felt bad that, during a time designed to unite us, I became focused on what I didn't have. But though I was uncomfortable with my emotions, I was grateful to have a time to be transparent about how I truly felt.

There were also times when I didn't want to be intimate because of the raw emotion I felt. I have always struggled with wanting to maintain control in various situations. Yet I remembered that God's grace is sufficient for me and His strength is made perfect in my weakness. God's grace is what allowed me to be vulnerable and express my true feelings and receive the comfort and strength I needed to keep healing.

Because of God's grace, I could feel the feelings and not keep them bottled in. Feeling my feelings allowed me to release my hurt from our miscarriage each time I hit a moment in which my loss felt insurmountable.

Just as my husband comforted me, God can and will comfort us during our time of need. He's simply waiting on us to tell Him how we truly feel. When we cast the load of our cares upon the Lord, we will receive His care in return *(Psalm 55:22)*.

PRAYER STARTER:

Lord, please help me to know that Your grace is here every single time that I need it. In receiving Your grace, I also receive Your strength. Please help me to cast my cares, anxiety, and load upon You and exchange them for Your stability.

Day 11

STILL PROCESSING

There is a time for everything,

and a season for every activity
under the heavens:

a time to be born and a time to die,

a time to plant and a time to
uproot,

a time to kill and a time to heal,

a time to tear down and a time to
build,

a time to weep and a time to laugh,

a time to mourn and a time to
dance…

—Ecclesiastes 3:1–4 NIV

In speaking to a few of my mom friends who'd experienced loss, I learned that their losses were extremely isolating. They were still processing or grieving their losses while their spouses had seemingly moved on. I remember feeling this as well. As a physician, my husband has been "trained" to deal with loss and grief. While he did emote about the loss of our child, he also knew how to move on. It's a part of his job and training, and I could not move on as quickly as he did. I didn't know how to deal with the differences in our ways of processing our loss, which made the loss even more painful.

I was reminded by a dear friend that men grieve differently and that just because he wasn't emoting the same way I was didn't mean the loss wasn't affecting him. As women, we carry our children in our bodies, which is different from a man's experience. This is your reminder that it's okay to still process and grieve even if it feels like your spouse has moved on. For me, grief would often be the most severe early in the morning or late at night. Tears would just begin to fall, and I couldn't stop them. Whenever tears come, let them fall. After all, you're still processing and it's all a part of your healing process. Without rain, flowers wouldn't grow.

PRAYER STARTER:
Lord, please help me to be patient during my grieving process. Please help me not to move past it or ignore it without embracing it. When I feel alone in my grief or feel like my spouse has moved on, please let me know that You are still here with me and I'm not alone.

Day 12

TRIGGERS

I have learned, in whatsoever state
I am, therewith to be content. I
know both how to be abased, and I
know how to abound…

—Philippians 4:11b–12a KJV

Triggers are unexpected. They lie dormant until someone or something activates them. They elicit a fight-or-flight, explosive-or-emotional response when you least expect it. I was triggered recently by a familiar situation, one I'd experienced in the past, that reoccurred in my present. Immediately, I became emotional and was reminded of the pain I'd felt long ago—the pain of abandonment, frustration, and feeling out of control. In that moment, I felt like a six-year-old little girl experiencing that hurt for the very first time.

When we are triggered, we have a choice. We can succumb to it or fight through it. Loss often breeds triggers, as do feelings of discontent, as Paul writes about in Philippians. It's easy to focus on what we are still believing God for, rather than focusing on what He has already blessed us with. As believers, we can choose to be content amid our loss. Contentment means that regardless of our situation, we can still choose joy. Does it mean we are happy with the situation? No. Does it mean we may have to fight daily or moment by moment to be content? Yes. Does it mean the trigger won't come back again? No. Does it mean that God will be with us when we're having familiar feelings of hurt, frustration, or grief? Absolutely!

PRAYER STARTER:

Lord, I was recently triggered by [insert trigger here]. Please carry me through my feelings of hurt, frustration, and grief. I will be anxious for nothing, but in everything by prayer and supplication, with thanksgiving, make my request known to You. And Your peace, which passes all understanding, will guard my heart and mind (Philippians 4:6–7). In Jesus' name. Amen.

YOU'RE STRONGER THAN YOU THINK

But he said to me, "My grace is
sufficient for you, for my power
is made perfect in weakness."
Therefore I will boast all the more
gladly about my weaknesses, so
that Christ's power may rest on me.

—2 Corinthians 12:9 NIV

Trauma has a way of making us feel like we won't make it. After we've been traumatized, unexpected events can make us feel helpless or like we're unable to cope.

The beautiful thing about being connected to God is that we can take on His strength during our times of weakness. It's a beautiful exchange in which we can rest in God's power and not our own. As our Creator and our Father, He knows what we need before we even ask. When you rest in His strength, you'll realize you're stronger than you think.

PRAYER STARTER:
Father, Your strength is made perfect in my weakness. Today I'm asking for an outpouring of Your strength. Please help me rest in and rely on You. I exchange my weakness for Your power. Amen.

RESILIENCY

He will never put more on you
than you can bear.

**—old adage (apparently adapted from 1
Corinthians 10:13)**

Whatever I have, wherever I am,
I can make it through anything in
the One who makes me who I am.

—Philippians 4:13 MSG

Sometimes what God thinks we can bear and what we think we can bear are polar opposites. Ofttimes God's definition of what I can bear sets the bar way too high for my liking, but then I think, He knows what He's doing, even if I don't.

As a child, I played with weighted inflatable toys that you knock down. No matter how hard you'd hit them, they would always bounce back up. Isn't it funny how life doesn't seem that way? We may get knocked down, but we don't always feel like we can get back up.

But God does.

I am reminded of Jesus' death and resurrection. It absolutely did not look like He would get back up. In fact, the women who came to prepare His body fully expected to find him lying in the tomb. But His death was not the end. Three days later, He rose with all power, and His resurrection power is living in each of us. All the onlookers of Jesus' death fully believed the crucifixion was the end—even his mother Mary did. As believers today, we have the advantage of knowing that Jesus' death was not the end, but only the beginning. What you're going through is temporary—the hurt, the grief and the pain. You will get through this. You are resilient. You are a fighter.

PRAYER STARTER:

Father, Your Word says, "Whatever I have, wherever I am, I can make it through anything in the One who makes me who I am" (Philippians 4:13 MSG). Help me to fight and make it through, no matter what.

LIVING LOSS

Then Jesus went to work on his
disciples. "Anyone who intends to
come with me has to let me lead.
You're not in the driver's seat;
I am. Don't run from suffering;
embrace it. Follow me and I'll show
you how. Self-help is no help at all.
Self-sacrifice is the way, my way, to
finding yourself, your true self."

—Matthew 16:25–26 MSG

Losing is quite humbling. As a child, do you remember team captains who would choose their teams? No one wanted to be the last pick, because it meant you weren't wanted. I was often the last pick due to my lack of athleticism.

The interesting thing about God is that when we suffer it's not because God has chosen us last, it's because He's chosen us first. In the book of Job, God asks Satan, "Have you considered my servant Job?" (Job 1:8 NIV). To be "considered" means that God has preselected us for a very great assignment. Jesus was chosen to suffer for the benefit of humanity. Job was selected because God had great faith in him. Think about it: God had faith in Job. He told Satan that there was "no one on earth like [Job]," he was a perfect and upright man, and he feared God (Job 1:8 NIV). It doesn't get much better than that. As a result, Job was chosen to suffer.

This concept is not popular, but it is true. To be tried by God is one of the greatest forms of flattery, but it can also be the most humbling. Jesus lost His life. Mary lost her Son. Job lost his family and his livelihood. Naomi lost her husband. Ruth lost her husband. Joseph lost his family. Yet they were chosen, preselected by God because they had the fortitude to suffer in loss while giving God glory. God chose them to suffer, and they chose God to lead them through it.

As God's children, we are not promised a life without heartache. Instead, we are promised that He will lead us through every situation.

PRAYER STARTER:

Lord, Psalm 34:18 tells me that You are "close to the brokenhearted and [save] those who are crushed in spirit" (NIV). I don't know why You chose me, but please help me to understand that You are with me and You see the bigger picture. Thank You for choosing me and thank You for giving me the strength to endure.

Day 16

CALLED TO BE A MOTHER

He has made everything beautiful
in its time. He has also set eternity
in the human heart; yet no one can
fathom what God has done from
beginning to end.

—Ecclesiastes 3:11 NIV

I was catching up with a friend who'd experienced the recent loss of a child. She shared that she knew she was called to be a mother—not through adoption, or by mothering someone's else's child, but by physically giving birth to a child. Her circumstances at the time revealed everything but that.

What do you do when your timing and God's timing don't align? For some, frustration sets in—doubt, worry, or unbelief. We might find ourselves really questioning if we heard God or if what we feel called to do or to be will really happen.

In the Bible, Sarah experienced the very same thing. God promised Abraham that he would be a father of many nations, yet Sarah and Abraham's circumstances revealed the exact opposite. How could two people in their elderly years have a son after the woman's womb had been barren for so long? Sarah wasn't certain about God's timing, so she took matters into her own hands.

A pastor of ours, Apostle Bertha F. Terry, has always said, "God's B plan is better than His A Plan," meaning that the second time God does something is always better than the first time. Jesus overcame the law. Moses was supposed to die, but Pharaoh's daughter saved him. Ruth and Naomi lost everything they had, but the Lord brought Boaz into their lives. God's B plan is always better than His A plan.

In waiting, our character gets perfected, and God's will is revealed. Is it always what we want? Not always. My friend is still waiting. But while she is waiting, she is living. Are things as she hoped? No. Is her life a beautiful depiction of God's story and grace, regardless of her not becoming a mother? Most definitely.

PRAYER STARTER:

Lord, please help me to line up my expectations with Your will for my life. In my waiting, please help me not to be discouraged. Please help me to look to the beautiful things You've placed in my life and the eternity You've placed in my heart. Today, I trust Your timing and ask for the strength to endure while waiting.

ARE YOU PREGNANT?

And they overcame him by the
blood of the Lamb, and by the
word of their testimony.

—Revelation 12:11 KJV

While my mom and my sister visited me after our miscarriage, I had a massage therapist come over to thank them for spending time with me. During the therapist's time in our home, she randomly asked if I was pregnant. It stunned me. It felt like daggers thrust into my heart. I told her no, and left it at that.

Later that evening, I shared with her that I had been pregnant but had recently miscarried. She, too, shared her personal story of a stillbirth. In that moment, I realized encouragement could come from the most unexpected places. She went on to share that she had just begun to be able to really talk about what had happened in the last few years. As much as we would like it to, grief doesn't have an expiration date.

While I did not appreciate her asking if I was pregnant, I was grateful for the encouragement that occurred as a result of me opening up. Everyone grieves differently, but if it helps to talk about what happened, do it. You may find more encouragement than you expect.

I love how the Lord always makes us realize that we're not alone. Even in grief.

PRAYER STARTER:
Father, thank You for surrounding me with people who understand what I am going through. When I feel alone, please remind me that You are right here with me.

Day 18

CONSIDERED BY GOD (PART 1)

Then the LORD said to Satan,
"Have you considered my servant
Job? There is no one on earth like
him; he is blameless and upright,
a man who fears God and shuns
evil."

—*Job 1:8 NIV*

To be considered by God is one of the greatest conundrums you can ponder. On one hand, it's an honor that the Most High has you on His mind, while on the other hand, it can be hard to accept this honor when you think about the Scripture verse quoted above. Job was considered by God, yet God gave the devil access to Job so that Job could be tried.

Yes, God gave Satan permission to try His servant Job. We often focus on the first part of the Scripture—the negative part that depicts this judge who is granting permission, essentially, for something bad to happen. Yet the most captivating part is why Satan was granted access to Job.

Job's character drew God to him. Job was blameless and upright and God knew that despite what came Job's way, Job would never shun Him. Isn't that amazing? The King of the universe had so much confidence in His servant that He granted Satan access to him to prove His point.

Did you know that God is confident in you? You can trust Him to carry you through this present storm. He is a very present help in time of trouble.

PRAYER STARTER:

Lord, thank You for considering me. Please help me to consider You, as You consider me, and help me to lean on You in the most trying times. While I don't understand everything that has happened and is happening, please help me to trust You despite all that I see. Thank you for trusting me.

Day 19

CONSIDERED BY GOD (PART 2)

Then the LORD said to Satan,
"Have you considered my servant
Job? There is no one on earth like
him; he is blameless and upright,
a man who fears God and shuns
evil."

—*Job 1:8 NIV*

I was recently watching a show on dog training. The family of the soon-to-be-adopted dog was planning to take him on family trips and needed to train him to operate without a leash. In order to do so, they tethered the dog to a thirty-foot leash, so that he could practice obeying their commands at a distance. Once he learned how to obey their commands from thirty feet away, the leash came off and he could go free under his owner's guidance.

This is the image that I see in Job 1. The sovereign God gives Satan access to Job, within reason, to try Job, to prove what God already knew about Job—that he was upright and blameless.

God also knew that despite whatever happened in Job's life, Job would not curse Him. Do you know that Job lost everything? His livelihood, his children, and so much more. Yet he never cursed God! After he was proven, Job was given double for his trouble.

When you consider what you're going through, know that our sovereign God has granted access for you to be proven. Everything is part of His plan, including the storm you're facing right now.

PRAYER STARTER:

Lord, even though I may not understand my current storm, please help me to trust Your will. We are not promised our lives will be without trials, but we are promised that You will be with us. Help me to remain tethered to You, in Jesus' name.

Day 20

REFLECTION OF YOU

For our light affliction, which is but
for a moment, worketh for us a far
more exceeding and eternal weight
of glory…

—2 Corinthians 4:17 KJV

Your loss is not a reflection of you—it is a part of your journey. During moments of grief, it's easy for guilt to set in. Your mind can wonder, "What if I had done this or that?" I even told myself, "Maybe if I had stressed less about work, or rested my body more, I wouldn't have had a miscarriage." I was too familiar with guilt and was often reminded by my husband, a physician, that it hadn't been a viable pregnancy. It wasn't me—the miscarriage was my body's way of telling me it wouldn't be able to sustain the pregnancy full-term. It seemed so plain when he explained it.

In 2 Corinthians 4:17, God promises that our light afflictions are but for a moment. While nothing seems light about miscarriage, God promises us His glory. If you're struggling with guilt today, you're not alone. Rest assured that there's nothing you could have done differently. You are not at fault, and you are not alone.

PRAYER STARTER:
Lord, I'm struggling with feeling guilty. Please remind me to rest in Your promises and know that even though I don't understand why, You knew this would happen all along. Help me to look forward to Your eternal weight of glory.

Day 21

PRAYING FOR YOUR SPOUSE

That is why we never give up.
Though our bodies are dying, our
spirits are being renewed every day.

—2 Corinthians 4:16 NLT

It's easy during loss to get caught up in how our loss impacts us. For those in relationships, it's easy to forget that the other person may be processing things too. I learned during our loss that my husband and I process grief very differently. While it didn't appear to me that he was grieving, he truly was. If you can muster up the strength to pray for your spouse, whisper prayers for understanding, so that while you both are handling your emotions differently, you'll have grace to sympathize with each other.

While you may not have the capacity to emotionally bear what your spouse is bearing, you can whisper prayers that God will provide the hope and comfort they need during an equally devastating time. As God extends grace to you, extend grace to your spouse, even if it seems that they are not grieving as you are.

PRAYER STARTER:

Lord, my spouse needs prayer just as much as I do. Please wrap Your loving arms around them and give them the strength, peace, and comfort they need, even when I can't. Please help us to extend grace to each other and communicate our feelings. Thank You for being our mediator and our peace. Please preserve our unity as we grieve and help us to be gentle with our words and actions. Help us to forgive as we desire others to forgive us.

Day 22

I CAN'T REMEMBER WHICH ONE

No test or temptation that comes
your way is beyond the course of
what others have had to face. All
you need to remember is that God
will never let you down; he'll never
let you be pushed past your limit;
he'll always be there to help you
come through it.

—1 Corinthians 10:13 MSG

A coworker of mine was missing from work for three to four days when I realized something was wrong. When I prayed for her, the Lord revealed to me that she had had a miscarriage. Little did I know that this was her third or fourth one. When we spoke, she couldn't even remember how many miscarriages she had had.

I had not yet experienced one. In the coming weeks and months, I would keep her encouraged and uplift her without knowing truly how she felt. What I did know was that God was faithful. And that He would not put more on her than she could bear. While that was easy to say, I'm sure it was much harder to endure. Have you ever experienced so much loss that you lose track? One loss bleeds into the next.

After this round of IVF, she wasn't going to try again. She wouldn't leave her life in limbo anymore, hoping a successful pregnancy would happen. The physical, emotional, and mental toil had become too much.

If you feel that you are at your breaking point, know that you serve a limitless God. He will take your limitless loss and make something beautiful out of it.

PRAYER STARTER:
Lord, I've lost count counting my losses. It seems like I'm losing more than winning. Please help me to know that for me to live is Christ and to die is gain. Please cover me mentally, physically, emotionally, and spiritually. Help me to trust in this unique demonstration of Your love.

EVERYONE IS GOING THROUGH SOMETHING

Bear one another's burdens, and so
fulfill the law of Christ.

—Galatians 6:2 NKJV

Grief made me more empathetic. In fact, trials can refine areas of our character. One of those areas can be how we respond to people.

My grief helped me to realize that everyone was going through something.

The day that I found out our baby didn't have a heartbeat, it took everything in me not to cry all the way out of the doctor's office. I remember catching the eye of an excited mom who had just seen her baby for the first time via ultrasound. The emptiness I felt in that moment was surreal.

I later recognized that same emptiness in another mother's eye. I recognized that look. I recognized the sorrow—and the anger.

Grief is perplexing. It can help you be more compassionate towards others, and it can also make you want to lash out at other people—people who don't, or maybe can't, understand what you're going through.

As we go about our day, it's important to remember that everyone doesn't know our situation, and since this is so, we may have to take a pause to gather ourselves together before we're able to respond to them in love.

PRAYER STARTER:

Lord, I have very little empathy for those around me right now. Please help me to respond in love when I don't feel like it.

WATERING YOUR JOY

They that sow in tears shall reap in
joy.

—Psalm 126:5 KJV

Trigger alert: DNC procedure.

Who knew that so many tears could eventually turn into joy? As I entered my DNC procedure room, and everyone began to pull on me and attach me to machines, tears began to fall. The wonderful nurse held my hand and shared that this was the part that made everyone cry.

She then went on to say that she too had had a DNC and that she cried every day for a month afterwards. In that moment, I found comfort in her words.

The beautiful thing about tears is that they are a promise joy will come. Not only does God bottle our tears, He promises that if we sow in tears, we will reap joy. It's hard to believe, but it really does happen. Now, as I'm sitting in the park with our two children and our brand-new rainbow baby, I'm reminded that joy does eventually come. I don't know what it will look like, but I know your joy is coming too.

PRAYER STARTER:

Lord, today I feel far from joy. As You bottle my tears, help me to be reminded that joy does eventually come. As your Word says, in Your presence is the fullness of joy and at Your right hand are pleasures forevermore (Psalm 16:11).

TAKE THE TIME

"Come to me, all you who are
weary and burdened, and I will
give you rest."

—Matthew 11:28 NIV

Healing takes time. After my DNC, I planned to take three days off work. My village encouraged me to take a week. I didn't understand why at the time, but after the procedure, I understood. Not only did I have to recover physically, I needed to recover emotionally, mentally and spiritually as well.

There's nothing like a crash course in loss to remind you you're not as strong as you think as you are. But that's the beauty of a God's grace. His grace is sufficient and His strength is made perfect in weakness. Regardless of the loss you've experienced, take the time you need to heal physically, mentally, emotionally, and spiritually. You'll be glad you did.

PRAYER STARTER:

God, I know Your grace is sufficient and Your strength is made perfect in my weakness. I feel very weak right now. Please visit me, see about me, and bestow Your grace on me. Help me to rest in You. In Jesus' name, amen.

Day 26

IF HE DOESN'T DO IT

Shadrach, Meshach, and
Abednego answered King
Nebuchadnezzar, "Your threat
means nothing to us. If you throw
us in the fire, the God we serve
can rescue us from your roaring
furnace and anything else you
might cook up, O king. But even
if he doesn't, it wouldn't make
a bit of difference, O king. We
still wouldn't serve your gods or
worship the gold statue you set up."

—Daniel 3:17–18 MSG

Friends of ours had been believing God for a baby for five years. As we sat across from them at the table, they shared that while they were an aunt and uncle, they desired to have their own child.

They had done everything—prayed, fasted, IVF, removed stressors, and so much more. Yet they had not been blessed with a child.

Something struck me that day as we were talking. They shared that while they were believing God for a child, if He didn't give them one, they would be the best aunt and uncle that they could be. That struck me. They knew God was capable, but if He didn't choose to bless them in the way they were asking Him to, they would be content.

Contentment can be a really challenging place to reach. Our hearts so long for what we have been petitioning God for, yet we have to honor that while He is God and can do it, He may not say "yes." No matter where you are on your journey, I pray that contentment would comfort you and hold you close to the heart of the Lord.

PRAYER STARTER:

Lord, Your Word says that Your ways are higher than our ways and Your thoughts are higher than our thoughts. Despite the fact that I don't understand all Your ways and thoughts, please help me to reach a place of contentment in You. Thank You for loving me more than I love the things I want to have right now. I love You.

LAZARUS, COME FORTH

"Father, if You are willing, take this
cup from Me. Yet not My will, but
Yours be done."

—Luke 22:42 Berean Standard Bible

The week between the initial ultrasound and the conclusive ultrasound confirming our miscarriage seemed like an eternity. I prayed the prayer "Lazarus, come forth" so many times, pleading with God to reverse what we had seen. I read, prayed, and fasted, hoping that God would change His mind.

Isn't it funny how we think that we can change God's mind? I have never had so much faith as I did that week, yet things did not work out as we hoped. The torment I felt was immeasurable. God, why didn't You do a miraculous work for me as You did for Lazarus? Finally, one night, God whispered to my heart, "Do you want My will?" At that moment, I could no longer argue.

Whatever the reason, it was not meant to be that the baby I had fallen in love with would be born at that time. In that moment, I needed grace to rest in God's sovereignty and not my own understanding. As Jesus said, I wish that this cup would pass from me, but not my will, but God's will be done (Matthew 26:39).

PRAYER STARTER:
Lord, I would love for You to reverse my situation. Please help me to rest in Your sovereignty instead of my understanding.

EXTRA TIME

To everything there is a season,

A time for every purpose under
heaven.

—*Ecclesiastes 3:1 NKJV*

When we found out we were pregnant again, I couldn't help but think how perfect God's timing was. Our family was in a good place, our kids were older, my career was in a better state, and my benefits at work allowed me to spend even more time at home bonding with our newborn. While I could not have possibly foreseen that a delay in our promise would be something to rejoice over, in hindsight, I was able to say, "God, you're good!"

Ivy, whose name means "God's gift," came just when God knew we needed her most.

She taught me that sometimes God withholds to bless all the more. Other times, it's simply not time yet. He may be waiting on a precise alignment of circumstances and His divine timing to release His divine blessing.

Isn't that how heaven will be? We won't know the specific time or season, but, in a moment, in the twinkling of an eye, we'll be caught up to see Jesus. That's the beauty of Ecclesiastes 3. We can rest assured that everything has a time and that there is a season for every purpose under heaven. Our times and seasons may not be God's, but rest assured that His plan is perfect. Until we receive His blessing, we wait.

PRAYER STARTER:
Lord, while I'm waiting, please help me to be patient. I pray for the perfect alignment of Your timing. Until then, I won't wait to live, I'll live while I wait.

Day 29

REMEMBERING

"When your children ask in time
to come, 'What do those stones
mean to you?' then you shall tell
them that the waters of the Jordan
were cut off before the ark of the
covenant of the Lord. When it
passed over the Jordan, the waters
of the Jordan were cut off. So these
stones shall be to the people of
Israel a memorial forever."

—Joshua 4:6–7 ESV

I remember thinking about how we would remember her—our unborn daughter. I had heard from several people how they chose to remember their angel babies. Some chose memorial candles, plants, or even jewelry. At first, I didn't see the value of that kind of thing, but then I saw the importance of honoring the moment—a moment that would forever be a part of my life and my story.

I chose to celebrate her by planting a blue hydrangea, our wedding flower. There was an image of an angel holding a baby hanging in our home, and it took on a new meaning for my family. Perhaps all along I was drawn to this image because God knew it would be part of my story.

Isn't it funny how God knows our journey before we do? While it can be disheartening to ask God why He allowed something to happen, it can also be comforting to know that He knew it would happen from the beginning. He is right there in the moment with us, providing everything that we need to conquer that moment.

To conquer it—not to forget it, but to allow it to strengthen us. Every time I walk by that image at the top of our stairs, I'm comforted in knowing that God knew all along. I receive hope in remembering my baby and knowing that I will meet her one day. I'm reminded that just as God brought my family through this, He will bring us through whatever comes our way.

This kind of remembering is just like what the Israelites were commanded to do in Joshua 4 above. The memorial stones represented the journey they endured, and served to remind them and their lineage of God's miraculous work in their lives.

PRAYER STARTER:
Lord, I find comfort in knowing that You knew this would happen all along. Help me to be okay with the outcome, even though I don't understand it. Please give me the strength to make it through.

Day 30

DEDICATED TO GOD

"Give, and you will receive. Your
gift will return to you in full—
pressed down, shaken together to
make room for more, running over,
and poured into your lap. The
amount you give will determine the
amount you get back."

—Luke 6:38 NLT

In the Bible, children are often dedicated back to God by their mothers. God blessed families with children and then the mothers returned them to God for His purposes and plans. Moses' mom had to give Moses back to God to spare his life; Mary had to give her teenage son to God and her adult son back to God to save mankind; Elizabeth had to give John back to God so that he could prepare the way for his cousin Jesus; Samson's mom had to let him go to fulfill the call on his life; Hannah gave Samuel to God to serve in the temple.

The interesting thing about these mothers is they were entrusted to raise their children for a season before dedicating them to God for service. For Hannah, it was only until Samuel was weaned; for Mary, it was until Jesus was twelve. Samson's mom had his childhood. Each of these women share a similarity: their devotion to God.

These women chose to instill in their children everything they needed for a life devoted to the One who'd empowered these women to carry life. As a result, the Lord was glorified in their children's lives.

However God chooses to bless us—whether it's by giving us children or not—it is His desire that we give our blessings back to Him. One thing that can be guaranteed is that we will experience life after loss. When we do, it is God's desire that we honor Him with the firstfruits of our new lives, dedicating His gift to us back to Him.

PRAYER STARTER:
Lord, thank You in advance for the life that I will experience after loss. Regardless of the blessing, please help me to dedicate back to You all that You've given me. Give me peace in the midst of what I don't understand. In Jesus' name. Amen.

CLOSING THOUGHTS

As your journey continues, my prayer is that this moment of loss becomes a memorial stone for you and your family, where you can reflect on the goodness of the Lord in the land of the living. It is my prayer that even when you feel inconsolable, the presence of God will overwhelm you—even in loss, may you find comfort, and may He show you that there will be life after loss. *"Weeping may endure for a night, But joy comes in the morning"* (**Psalm 30:5 NKJV**). I'm praying for your morning to come.

Yours in Christ,
Joinné Chandler

P.S. I would love to stay connected and learn how your story unfolds. Let's connect on IG @joinne_chandler or lifeafterlossbook.org. #lifeiscoming